P9-CAR-972

go early into the unknown

With love
from Pam
to Manjiri —

Pamela Armstrong

go
early into
the unknown

PAMELA ARMSTRONG, PH.D.

© 2010 by Pamela Armstrong
Printed in the United States of America

All rights reserved. No part of this publication may be reproduced or
transmitted in any form or by any means, electronic or mechanical,
including photocopying, recording, or by any information storage and
retrieval system, without the prior written permission from the publisher
or the author. Contact the publisher for information on foreign rights.

ISBN: 978-0-9842668-9-0

acknowledgments

So many people have made it possible for me to create this book.

First and foremost, I want to thank my daughter Megan Armstrong Wills for the moral support she gave to me throughout this process. Somehow through all the calamities and errors of my life, she stands by me.

My sister Valeria Bateson was a crucial advisor and editor as I was creating the poems and shaping them into cohesive groups. She has a brilliant eye for words and the deeper messages conveyed in literature. She and her wonderful husband Nicholas Bateson are sponsors, and have made a huge difference in bringing this book to publication.

My friends Jack McCoy and Mike Hendry have been very supportive and honest in their feedback about the poems as I wrote them, and I treasure their opinions as creative people who love writing.

L Douglas St. Ours has been an inspiration to me throughout the last few months, as he writes almost every day. He shares his work online and engages in dialogue with friends about his life and his work. He has generously invited me, a fledgling poet, to readings and encouraged me to keep going.

I also want to thank Ken Rochon who has been a relentless coach throughout the process. He is skilled at swift kicks to the posterior, and these were vital to me. Ken introduced me to Carolyn Sheltraw who is great at design and layout, and to Vincent E. Sharps of Graphic Press. Vince was a committed partner in getting this book done.

Finally, I want to thank all my friends and family members who have supported the book by placing early orders and generally cheering me onward! This includes the Facebook friends who gave me comments and in some cases helped me to tweak the wording.

For my daughter,
Megan,
the brightest star
in my firmament

contents

I. ARTISTIC EXPRESSION AND THE CREATIVE PROCESS

on fire 3

urge to merge 6

ones and ciphers 8

gone 12

could 14

evanescent. 16

II. GROWING UP AND GETTING OVER IT

go early into the unknown... 23

position 28

anything 34

get past 41

kind of mind. 45

III. GENERATIONS

taller 51

wait 54

how long 58

old school 61

treasure of the eternal kind 63

IV. STALLED IN THE FAST LANE

crowded passage .71

out of mind 75

reckless 78

well meaning 83

V. THE HEALING POWER OF NATURE

the ridge 91

blossom 95

ride the river down 98

blissful 101

on Porthcurno Beach 103

VI. THE MIXED BLESSING OF CLOSENESS

dicey. 109

cake 112

the tree 115

the spark. 119

close 123

am I 127

would. 129

so 133

VII. LETTING GO

which? 137

the desired state 140

easy go 145

by and by 148

VIII. THE GREATER GOOD

the front and back. 155

icon 158

end game 164

strange game. 169

assassins 173

long walk with a smoke. 176

the body politic. 181

artistic expression

and

the creative process

on fire

the fuse has
been lit now,
there is only
the need

to respect
the explosive
force to come

and your instinct
to back away,

your urge
to douse what
has been started

can no longer
be yielded to,
as you have

caved in,
frozen in fear,
debated in
two voices,
and cooked up
every cockeyed
watered-down
excuse~

this became
a bad act that
bores even you...

you need to
face the
music now,

and if you're
not ready for
the solo

at least
play a duet~

where your part
is the one people
remember

the fire
is the
heat,
the excitement
and the power

it is also
the only warmth
in a cold world

so cozy up
to it...

urge to merge

not sure what that is
but whatever that is
I want to be drawn to it,
to be mystified by it

dumbstruck and fascinated,
to become its captive
to step way down into it
with my hip boots

to take a long slow deep dive
and roll down and around in it,
to get into a blender with it,
to breathe only when it breathes

to get quite lost in it,
to lose my pointless life in it,
to thank it for showing me
exactly what I need to do

to forget what time it is with it,
to forget my age with it,
to forget to eat with it,
to not need sleep with it

to not care anymore with it,
to not feel hurt with it,
to escape their world with it,
to build my world inside of it

it is after all my sun and moon
and fills up all the emptiness~
I know I have to drown in
something, and this will be okay

∞

ones and ciphers

from the brain
to the heart
to the gut

to the fingers
to the keyboard
to the memory

all the poet
is saying
becomes

ones and ciphers
somewhere
in an unseen space

and as ephemeral
as the idea,
the mood,

the train of thought
wants to run
off the rails

but silently~
with no crash,
not even a whimper

just slip-
sliding away
into the ether

never to be
recovered
from the
random fragments

that bounce
around in
the chamber
of awareness

it surfaced,
it bloomed,

it became
almost coherent

saved as a draft~
then a draft
came along

and blew
the paper
under the door

out into
the maelstrom
where it was
chewed up

and made
into a
word salad,
chopped fine

with all those
other wondrous
thoughts that

got lost in
the translation…

∽

gone

schedules
time frames
logistics
deadlines
no watch
no calendar

goals
duties
chores
obligations
margarita

checkbooks
check boxes
check lists
scribble

voice mail
email

snail mail
off the grid

chain letters
spam
unwanted solicitations
can't find me

need you
want you
you have to be here

I need me
I want me
I couldn't find me
I have to be here

And my
itinerary?
It's itinerant.

could

could I ride along
in the current
created by your smile

could I borrow
some of the heat
created by your brilliance

could I sidle up
to the pull of
your magnetic energy

could I take a side
glance into the depths
of your perception

could I have the
leftovers from your
love for humanity

could I just make up
stuff about what
is in your heart

could I ease your
pain without making
an incision

could I hook up with
your soul without
draining its essence

could you give me a
simple subtle signal
to say you don't mind

on the other hand
could you leave me
hanging blissfully
in
sus
pense

∽

evanescent

open up like
it's okay
that what
you release
will change
and drift away

travel like
there will be
fuel for
your next
few miles
in the most
unlikely place

sing like
there is no
point at all
but the next

tune and lyric
coming to mind

dance like
all your
energy and
being are in
love with the
next move

speak like
your words
will reach
the far shore
of all that
we know

guess like
your
imagination
shifts the
edge of all we
don't know

see like
you are
aware of
shape and
color for
the first time

listen like
the sounds
are long-lost
messages
being revealed

soothe like
you can bring
great comfort
to all you see

harmonize
with the small
and simple
so the power
of peace
seeps from
your pores

give love like
it's surplus
merchandise
approaching
its pull date

sleep like
you are
cradled in
loving arms
that won't ever
let you go

growing up
and
getting over it

go early into the unknown…

standing in the kitchen,
there was an
urgent sense
that time was a
speed boat~

and the thought of
being pulled along
behind it on skis
did not appeal

an impatient girl,
I yearned
for the helm

though I managed
to spin out the old
Beetle in my first outing
with Dad riding shotgun

in overdrive,
I envisioned myself
as powerful, for no
particular reason

passing the driver's test~
even though the
gentleman called me
a lead foot

so eager to zoom
down the road
to undefined but
limitless destinations

and due caution
was, in my mind,
a swamp filled with
reason, logic and the
absurd notion of
self-knowledge

many said
I would go far,
but at seventeen

there was
no compass

the future was
magnetic north
and I called it out,
invited it to show itself

and I was suddenly
aware of my metallic jumpsuit
with a locked-up zipper

whoosh-swept up in
crazy down-south college
nineteen sixty-two

that story started
all too soon- stranded
hundreds of miles
away from that kitchen

with strangers
huddled around the
black and white TV

with our President
telling us about the
missiles pointed
directly at our dorm~

first big clue that
the placid Eisenhower
fifties of our sock hops
were way over

and the world was
way bigger
than an oyster

and the natural
predators were
not confined to
a restricted zone,
but roamed freely~

what was a girl
to do but write
positive letters home

and believe in
magnetic north...

⬡

position

being a sidebar
or a parenthesis
is not so bad
as being a
question mark
in your own mind~

being a being
requires being
really asleep
so you can be
really awake

to be really asleep
you need
to feel safe~
to feel safe you
need to be
the Protector's child

when really awake
you need to be
really present,
like a blessed child
on Christmas morning

to be in awe and
wonder at all the
things that you
are discovering
about the world,
yourself and others

you are present
with yourself
when you
embrace your
five senses~

you breathe
into your body
and are aware of
feeling good,
bad, or in between

you learn what is
and is not okay
with you

you read your gut
and express it
"for what it's worth"

you learn the
limits of reality
and the boundaries
with others

you learn to talk
to yourself so that
you are not trapped
in those moods

you learn how to
calm and soothe
yourself so you
can be less extreme

you learn to
feel grateful for
the things you
took for granted

you learn to trust
yourself and respect
the fingerprint
that you are

you learn to treasure
and develop the
gifts you are given

you learn to accept
that luckily
others are not
like you~

but that is
not a personal,
intentional slight
or abandonment

you decide that others
are worth the hassle~
even though you hate
being fair to them

you learn to make
requests when
you are upset
or disappointed

you learn that being
right can make
your life a
lonely road

you learn that we are
all good and bad,
and that you are
not here for a contest

you learn that
the past is
to learn from,
but we build
from today

you learn to
star in your
own show
and measure
yourself by your
own standard

always remembering
that love is the fuel
of all meaning
and all
meaningful success

anything

in those heady days~
when wringer washers
were replaced
by washing machines

and the ironing
became less than
an all-day affair~

a new world opened
up for my parents,
the devout
do-it-yourselfers~

they could relax,
play music,
read and dream

and the future
looked rosy

to those children
of the Depression

the sky was the limit—
we lucky kids
were sure to
find sweet success

we nodded and
wondered what
that meant

my sister and I
were not
headed for the
Ivy Leagues

nor were we
raised just to
"marry well"

for careers,
the rhyme went
"doctor, lawyer"

for women, it was
type and file,
nurse the sick,
or teach

we happened to
be smart, but
that might be
an affliction

one must
land a catch
to avoid the
shame of being
an "old maid"

we smiled sweetly,
and I being the
dreamy inattentive
type of girl

played out my
mixed feelings to
the max~

drove too fast,
clowned around,
acted crazy,
prided myself on
getting less than
stellar grades

I kept thinking—
gee, I can do anything,
but how do I get
there from here

and the straight-
laced guidance
counselor had
the nerve

to be vague about
my possibilities,
and downright
discouraging to
my talented sister

saying "oh, you
don't want to
be an architect,
you'll have to climb
on tall buildings"

with no access to
good advice,
I threw in the towel
along with a
monkey wrench~

skipped my
senior year,
left our safe
small town,
went off to
the U. of Huge~

getting
lost in the
social
insanity

of southern
sorority girls and
frat boys, mixed
with New Yorkers
and Jersey kids

who felt free
to heavily
spike the punch,
throw big
make-out parties

sell each other speed
to pull all-nighters,
and generally
run amok

I did figure out
I wanted to
major in psych~

with no idea how
long and hard
that journey
would be~

but the seeds
of who I became
showed up in that
scared freshman

and I can count on
the survivor inside~

I think I had to lose
myself first to find
that later...

∞

get past

the next thing,
the next big thing
was all that mattered~

swept up in the
drive to avoid
standing still

afraid to be mired
in instructions
of others

wanting to
fly free~
ignore the limits

I was here to seek,
to find, not to
study or know

don't bog me down
with rules and
the history of things

as I might
never get secure
enough in those

I am secure in my
gut, my instinct
to discover

things others
may never
understand

others found me
way too intense,
unable to
justify that

now the starkness
of loss
has softened me

love is more urgent,
seeking too
lonely

I seek now
the past and
what shaped me

points where I
wandered or was
pulled off course~

not knowing,
of course, what
off course was

seekers must
go down many
blind alleys

but eyes must be
open to see
they are blind

possibility lives
in the most
dire places

but may meet a
violent death at the
end of the alley

I can see
moving too fast
and too far

blinds me to
the beauty
of where I
came from...

∞

kind of mind

the more I
studied the brain
the less I knew

the more I
analyzed
my thoughts
the less I
could change them

the more I felt
for others
the less they
seemed to
feel for me

the more I cried~
seeking solace~
the less friends
found to say

the more I stayed
with those of
"like mind"
the scarier my
big decisions looked

the more I feared
those unlike me
the less I saw
their potential
to teach me

by always seeking
my comfort zone
I was stuck in molasses

It took about a year
to clean my shoes

so the more I spent
time with myself
the less afraid
I was to be close

the more I looked at
my best moments
the less I wanted
to trade places

the less I hated
the mirror
the more I loved the
stories told in it

the less I
blamed others
the more I forgave
them and me

the less lonely I was
the more
I saw
I'm good company

good company
attracts good company
of the most
fascinating kind

I do not need them...
I just prefer
being with their
kind of mind

＊

generations

taller

a little boy
proudly steps up
to the scale

demanding to
see what's
happening

his height
keeps going
up and up

a big smile-
a great thrill
to get proof

that all the
growing pains
and effort

are paying off~
giving him a shot
at greatness

he doesn't need
to know what
greatness means~

better for him
to think it
comes as part
of the same
boxed set

with doing the
right things
over and over~
caring for himself
and caring
about others

as he grows,
the view will change
and the man

will define his own
idea of greatness...

⚬

wait

you're so hyper,
so impatient,
you just need
to wait

wait for Dad~~
he is mad cause
Mom's mad,
he is in his cave
and you'll get
punished later

wait for Mom~~
she is grading
papers, saving
for your college,
mending your jeans

wait for sis~~
she has locked the

door of her secret
studious
sophisticated
life

wait to learn~~
you're a
lazy student,
you need to
be spoon fed,
don't ask all
these questions

wait to shine~~
your muse is at
your elbow
but you are not
tuned in, and
she is not amused

wait to say the truth
to all your friends~~
they are not that loyal,
they will stand against you

wait to risk~~
to fail makes you
a loser, and losers
are all zeroes,
they live in Loserville

wait to love~~
your heart is on
your crying sleeve,
no doubt it will
get crushed

wait to live~~
you must bend to
others, or you'll be alone,
and that is worse than death

wait to lead~~
the young have no real
voice, they have
crazy notions and
the world is deaf

wait to wait~
wait to stagnate~

the world will keep
you waiting later
many many times

we know some things
just can't be rushed

but being
a waiter is
not what you
had in mind...

how long

how long can you
sit on a fence~

raising a child
without taking
a stand,

without
sketching
a map

to help guide
those unsure
feet on
treacherous
ground

how long
can you avoid
the gaze

of the child
who hears
what you say,
but sees
what you do

how can
you not
take in
that innocence

so precious-
and needing
protection,
connection,
direction

do you not
see the
gift in this
experience

can you not
put aside your own
self-centered agenda

just enough so that
you see your life's
measure....

and the emptiness
of getting older,
even with botox

when your child
does not even
know who you are...

old school

what was
and is
no longer

is not
to be
retrieved

as each
decade
becomes
ancient
history~

the speed
of change
makes one
feel retro~
obsolete

but the
tribal elders
continue to
speak

even when
nobody listens…

and they
whisper
their
wisdom

to those
whose ears
are deafened

by the best
earphones
money can buy…

∽

treasure of the
eternal kind

you dropped into
my story line
just in time

as I was
trending
toward a

hard-working,
otherwise
hedonistic,
way of life

and trying
not to face that
serious watershed
at age 30

when the party
so often is
a waning moon

and the denial
of youth stands
in jeopardy

the body speaks
in a loud voice,
telling of

the steady onward
march of that
dang life cycle

and somehow
the joys of
freedom began
to feel overrated

luckily my girlfriend
had a due date
the same week as mine

and there was
a great feeling
of connection

as our generation
was the first
to have assurance
that we could delay

and we moved
forward, embracing
the challenge~

to keep our careers
and our identity

while nurturing
diapering
soothing
and cooing

at our daughters
(as it turned out)
the girls who would
(we thought)

build on the
freedom and
empowerment
we felt in the 60's

you of course
had another
agenda in mind

as you grew,
you held up a
mirror to what
I said, what I did

and you called me
on it, even at the
age of three

you were such
a doll that I
of course melted
when you smiled

you loved words~
absorbed and
repeated so many

you weathered
confusing circumstance,
so many changes

and I floundered
so many times
that I weep to think

lost in the wilderness
of impending
divorce

somehow in
the darkest hours
you kept me going

reminding me
it was up to me
to build our future

I hate to think
what I'd be like now
without the strength
you demanded of me

you in turn
became my teacher
and I remain in awe
of the steely strength
you show

not from magical
empowerment,
but from knowing
who you are

and clearing
your own honest path
in this crazy life…

∽

**stalled
in the
fast lane**

crowded passage

fear enjoys
setting up housekeeping
in the neural pathways

when these
could otherwise be
pleasant places

when fear signs
a long-term lease,
they become
torturous

the instinct
is to wall off,
clam up

dread unknowns,
anticipate the worst,

and see others
as a threat to

the requirement
of keeping things
the same, or at
least under control

and it feeds on
itself, expands its
reach so that
small concerns
look bigger

suddenly you
are a Lilliputian
without back-up
and no plan

everyone has on
big shoes and
you are bound to
be stepped on

you do not
look forward to
being excited-

it feels too
much like
fear

and you seek
the company
of those who
help you stay
stuck in sameness

you put on the
brakes and fear
the power of the
accelerator

without
momentum,
the steering
wheel can
not move freely
and you no

longer have the
simple joy
of the wind
in your hair

the spaced-out
pleasure of
the countryside
whizzing by

and you find
it so hard
to escape

the fear of
the next
time fear
visits you
in that
tight little
space...

out of mind

it's in dim light
concealed
in shadow

lost in
the dust balls
just out
of reach

the bad that
haunts me
is blurry,
cold and
steel hard

a grainy
photograph
after a flood

the mean ones
are without face
and cannot be
summoned

the reasons
encrypted
in a child's
dream that
melted as the
sun rose

somehow
the pit
rises up
and swallows
the story

the story that
could free
me from
the bleak
lonely landscape

of rotting fruit
hidden in
shadows
spoiling the
bounty
of today

∽

reckless

so why is it
that I'm least
likely to know

the whereabouts
in my small domain
of the documents

that show the
info they want~
that prove
so many things

things that others
ask for in times
of dire need
or disaster

things a more
cautious person

might have stored
on a microchip

filed in digital
folders in
alpha order

when in somber
reflection~ at times
I realize these are
tickets for the gate

and where in the
hockeysticks are
those tickets

without them I'll
be disallowed,
excluded and way
past the deadline

I can wear excuses
like a charm bracelet
and the guards at the
gate still won't smile

in a fascist state
I'd be herded
into a truck
never to appear again

because I forgot
my homework
I forgot to be afraid~
their vice grip slipped my mind

but I think like a free person
and therein lies the problem
not just free but
blessed by good fortune

in that way
I am a wistful child
living in the vapors
of her imagination

a Blanche DuBois
who hasn't hit
bottom and doesn't
think one exists

a pollyanna who
can make things
happen or go away
in her innocent fog

as paperless polly
I'll be fumbling
for the data to make
wrenching calls

the go-or-no-go
calls that beg
to be made when
facing the big red
binary switch

see, Father Time is just
a made-up character
in a boring book
I never read

the rules should be bent
to accommodate
my exempt status
after all, I'm a good person

but the facts are not
endlessly open for
the editor's pen

and I lack the power
to blur what
is absolute~
the decisions
of Solomon

so I vow to
pack light now
be ready to fly with only
three ounces of liquid

because I hate structure,
I will pretend
I'm actually
packing for you.

well meaning

sometimes we
sign up for
bad bargains

the kind that
reach up and
take a big bite
out of you

the kind that
cause buyer's
remorse
later

when
we're trying
to avoid
bleeding out

some pain is
just downright
familiar,
and we're
more hopeful
this time

the pain of the
new relationship
is "not as bad"
as that other one

the pain of the
habit, the
hangovers,
the burned-out
nerve endings

the glossed-over
loneliness
and disappointment

the paradox of
feeling unloved
by our habit

and in the end
unlovable

is no longer
an issue
because
feeling good
dropped off
the options list

now we are
living to prove
a point, and
to say "that's
okay, I can take it"
to say
"I didn't need
much anyway"

friends don't
seem to get
how intimate
it is to be
bonded by
what was

a reasonable
substitute or
almost workable

they're not
inside the habit-
the need, the
empty gulf of
wish and want and
need and have to

they're not
inside the rage
concealed by
"No, I'm not angry"

the habit
wakes up each
day and strengthens
all by itself, to
protect us from
the burning
rays of truth

the same
rays that
could reveal
the beautiful
possibility
just ahead

real love forces us
to tell the truth
about what we
choose,
as we mean well
but took another
wrong turn...

the healing
power of
nature

the ridge

in the Carolina
mountains
a beautiful stream
rushed down
over a bed of
smooth stones

in a deep
forest
grove

its entrancing
sound brought
comfort~

a place of
rest from
the hard
uphill hike

that summer
day in my
sixteenth year

suddenly a
profound
connection
washed
over me

a new awareness
of the love
shown
in nature

the
beauty of
things not
spoiled by
pavement

the forever
feel of
the stream

my eyes opened
to the meaning of
my life's journey~

the awesome
solitude of
decisions to
be made~

my spirit
reached a
turning point
that day

and began
a journey
of discovery

as I feel
and express
the love

that came
to me there

and as I
didn't want
to leave it,
it never left me..

∞

blossom

how tender you are~
a fair flower
who hardly
experienced
more than
a rainstorm

your fragrant petals
intact and opening
in harmony with
the seasons and
the reliable sun

you do not cower
in the shadows
but spring up
with vigor ~
eager to meet
the first light of day

fearing not
to show your colors
no matter how
vivid, garish,
or unusual

flaunting your
beauty to those
who only want
to clip you for
a crystal vase

or sully your
purity, drink your
sweet nectar
and move on

you stand tall
and welcoming—
an open
expression of
the divine
paintbrush

fearing not
your mortality,
as you were
never taught
to hide

you are
the innocent
embodiment of
beauty for
beauty's sake

how can we
not melt in
your presence~
not only for
the gift you give
our eyes~

but for
playing out
the fleeting
transcendence
of this moment...

༄

ride the river down

born as a drop
turned to a trickle
running down to
a tiny stream

never tiring
never ceasing
joining in with
other streamlets
moving whatever
stands in our way

finding a groove
finding a weak place
finding a way to
go down, down

like tiny branches
lead to the limb
lead to the mighty trunk

we keep finding others
and linking, linking
combining our power
as a single force

carving out earth
carving out rock
carving out bigger
And bigger grooves

we follow the path
downstream to
we know not where
and do not care

we see bridges
we see levees
we see dams
we do not care

we know the best
way to go
and we will make
new land, new fruits,
new creations from

what was picked up
along the way

we do not rest
until we've found
our birthplace,
Mother Ocean,
who welcomes the
nice tall drink of
what was and what will be~

∽

blissful

how warm and snug and fitting
it feels as we are sitting
basking in the filtered rays
of spring's best light

welcomed by the wisteria
that has climbed bravely
up and across the arbor
after rising from the dead
of a three-blizzard winter

the sun backlights
big white puffs
that move with
stealth and grace
across the brilliant
rejoicing sky

time stretches in luxury
as a cat from a nap

and conversation flows
easy as connection
blossoms in the garden…

⟳

on Porthcurno Beach

so small~
to stand
among these
great boulders

a giant has
carelessly
flung down
towards the
crescent beach

an ancient stream
flows back and forth,
threading its way
among the rocks

a soothing sound
to harmonize with
the crash of
azure waves below

as fresh water
encounters the
last stretch of sand
it drops from sight
as I yearn to~

running deeply,
tirelessly to that
moving line of
demarcation

where sea and
shore meet
in a quick
embrace~

wind and mist
have given way
to September sunshine
and a light breeze

a table has been
set for me
on a flat rock
sheltered by granite cliffs

my senses receive
the beauty so
graciously on display
for my visit

my spirit enters
Cornish time
in this
snug harbor

I am reminded
here of truths
no longer willing
to be pushed aside

I am reminded here
of the links
I have
to what is timeless

⚭

the mixed
blessing of
closeness

dicey

for a man,
you have all
the powers
of a siren

your voice says
come hither
no matter what
else you may mean

stripped of all
power to reason,
naked,
unhinged

I show nothing,
for you may
have great
power to destroy

and fiddle
while my
naive spirit burns

in myth
I'd call on
faeries to
make you mute

so I might
see you with
my other
senses

and yet
my grieving
ears would
turn away

not to
know again
where I was
going

but to hear
the lovely
sound of
other
promises…

∞

cake

love with no icing,
no fancy glaze
or filling

sweet is an
acquired taste
that can blow
out your taste buds

then you can
no longer
notice the
beauty of the
unadorned

the subtle flavors
of what is
natural and of
the earth

you cannot savor
the complex
texture of
really good love

you are bowled
over by the
camouflage at
the surface

you keep looking
for that perfect
bite of love,
pack your cheeks
with the "good stuff"

you take the
leftovers home
and cannot
get enough,
as you didn't
get that bite

you wonder
why the

sweetness left
you wanting more,
needing more

If you picked
fancy over basic,
you may need
to check who
decided what
the difference was~

the tree

blown off the tree
by a strong wind
when you were only a bud

you somehow
found soil to
take root in

you might be
a bit harder
around the edges,

have a somewhat
less than perfect complexion,
just a few splotches

but hardy you are,
unscathed by
harsh winters

you may be
greedy,
needing
lots of room

for your roots
to spread out~
to have no
rivals close by

you had to
dig so deep
as a young thing
just to keep going

the struggle was
lonely~
your scraggly self
not noticed

and now you
have a suspicious,
smiling neighbor

who has
tended the
earth you cling to
with your gnarly roots

you find that
disquieting,
even a threat,
because what
is given can vanish

you need the
clay, the rocks,
the grit
to feel at home

and yet the
silky topsoil
has perfect texture

it glistens in the sun,
soaks in the
rain, it is so rich

the mulch is that
final proof~
someone tends
this garden

telling
passersby:
this is a
loving home

to your surprise
your grit
is not unwelcome

and your
story
gives depth
to this landscape...

the spark

so now
these
cell walls
are starting
to soften

as we discover
what shaped us
what soothes us
what shakes us
what moves us

what allows
our boundaries
to become
porous to
each other

what blends
we can make
from the
special hues
of color

that we
have mixed
to express
who we are

that we took
great pains
to perfect

so they stand
out on our
beautiful
solitary palette

sometimes a
masterpiece
is created on
top of another

or the key
elements combine
to form a collage
of mutual meaning

this can feel like
a surprise attack
on our sense of
history, ownership,
and pride

but surrendering
allows me
to dissolve
into a brand
new medium

of we-ness,
not subtracting
from my impact,
my essence

a medium that
reshapes

my ideas of
strength and
weakness

and prompts
the smile that
slowly spreads
across my face

when we are
playing in
the box of paints,
making new names
for our shared
experiences…

∞

close

close without the c
seems so easy
to achieve

just missing one
letter, replaced
by question marks

that one recipe
no one shared,
the secret of the Grail

the quest for
what may
endure

the slings and
arrows of
circumstance,

the changes
leading to the
inevitable~

the wise sherpas
have died
and left us

with only the
metaphors and
assurances

mapped out
in holy books
and philosophy

yet the heart
yearns to
be open~

so weary of
guarding the
injured spirit~

and needing
to be seen,
to inspire wonder

as the first
glimpse of
another galaxy

and like a
force of
nature

it does not
turn in
upon itself,

but makes
its presence
known

requesting
forgiveness

like the earth
forgives an
earthquake

the heart
is alive when
it creates

what will last,
with one
extra clause

providing special
instructions
in the event

that emergency
drills are needed
in the quake zone...

∞

am I

if I am
what you say,
then what am I
when you
aren't here?

if I do
what you say,
then what do I
do when you
don't say?

if I am as good
as your last
look, then
what good am
I when you
don't look?

if I am less
than I was
before,
what does
all this add
up to?

☙

would

would you
sacrifice all
for the sake
of love

would you
dumb down,
smarten up,
suit up,
transform

would you
hang around,
be at his
beck and call

would you
ask around,
memorize his

favorite
everything

would you
pal around,
do things
you really
despise

would you
stick around,
starve cause
he needs
you skinny

would you
mess around,
take up
a brand
new vice

would you
move around,
shed your stuff

and sail toward
the setting sun

would you
fool around,
take risks
that could
kill or jail you

would you
skirt around,
avoid the
sticking
points

would you
go around
saying what
you won't
say to him

would you
joke around,
hide what

you need
behind a smile

would you
see around
the next
corner to
where all
this leads…..

so

so soft
the spirit
that is love

so true
the heart
that is loyal

so strong
the bond
that is chosen

so sweet
the smile
that is shared

so natural
the face
that is secure

so rich
the harvest
of devotion

so peaceful
the warrior
who puts down
his sword

so relieved
the eyes
of forgiveness

so alive
the feeling
of friendship

so fearless
the commitment
to forever

letting
go

which?

death, life...
not necessarily
in that order
one is longer,
one closer,
so which one wins?

spark, no spark
please explain
how can we be
and then not be...
a magical force
exists and exits

the body left
is a cold shell
that once contained
a vibrant being, a
rolodex of
meaning, memories

this
seems a
vapor, a figment,
a dream, a layer
of awareness
falling into
no awareness

a favor
done for our
overactive
overambitious
demanding minds
that never seem to
know what's enough

that never can
put a real period
on a sentence
and mean it...

this seems
maddening
and even cruel
as we struggle

to define
the midpoint,
the endpoint

and yet it may
be so easy to
float and drift
away from all
the urgent and
unending stress
of the to do list
and the possibilities

endings may
be beginnings~
and there may
be relief in that~
but then
who cares if
we lose our edge?
...but then what
good are edges
without freedom?

the desired state

how tricky to
be human…

to seek so
many things
that don't
exist

and things
that cannot
last

my quest in my
extended youth
was to escape the
bonds of what
others predicted,

to compensate
for what

seemed so
wrong in me

with creative
stealth, the
outside obstacles
were easier
to overcome

succeeding
gave me a rush
which, when
in the solitude
of my own
company,

did not
translate
into feeling
at peace
with myself

by default
I'd go on
autopilot

and pretend

or even
sleepwalk
through
years of
my life

staying in
failed
relationships
and smiling

while
harboring
resentment,

unable to
walk away~

misguided in
medicating myself
to swallow
the feelings

hiding my
dilemma
from those who
cared about me

my desired
state was to
avoid conflict
to keep from
being alone

but now I
have found
the richness
inside myself

and share it
more freely
with others

I can
be whole
without the
"other half"

and I trust
fate to
determine
the rest...

༼༽

easy go

this time it
only caused
a misty kind of
sentiment

the kind that
happens when
you've been
touched by
something,
someone

it is not
a deep sea
dive, only
a glimpse

of what is
sparkling and
vividly alive

right under
the surface

it is right there
all the time,
to partake in-
it is not a
single event

it only hurts bad
when we
try to make it
a story

if "tune in tomorrow"
is the frame
then the
twists and turns
feel smooth

as we are not
really the author
of relationships

but one of the
characters
who may stay
or move on

and we need to
swim with the
fishes to find
the school
for our
next lesson...

❧

by and by

told to let go,
but where was
that instruction
manual

it seems
easy for some,
automatic

no tears,
no trauma,
just smooth
and silent

some have
felt burdened
by my tears

I should
find it

embarrassing

I should not
be so
weak

I should
seek peace
from a
stronger faith

I should
take a
chill pill

I should
use my
common
sense

I should
say
life goes on

but I cry
because
I love

to feel
the
connection

and the
risk that
goes with it

even singing
in the closeness
of a childhood
campfire

the wonder
of being
here together
is a truth
to be lived
openly

no longer
seeking comfort
behind that
wall

no longer
saying
I should
not need

no longer
being the
warrior on
the surface

no longer
hiding the
vulnerable
underbelly

but leaning
my head on
your shoulder,

saying
thank you
for being here...

to help me
let go

the

greater

good

the front and back

standing above
those down below~
you can see
their weakness

they can see
your power,
your perfection

you cannot
imagine needing
the way they need

you cannot
relate to their
helpless state

you would
be ashamed to
be seen with them

you would
rather die
than be
one of them

if you would help
them, it would
be a check by mail

but to meet their
gaze, to grant
them worth
and dignity

is far beneath
you, and so
you suffer
voluntary
blindness

for just as
the front and
back of the hand
need each other

the needy have
something to give,
something to teach
the needless

it's time to
sign up for
the lessons…

to be needed
lifts up the spirit
and gives joy~

which so often
the needless
cannot find..

∞

icon

what fame
did was
scramble up
the image
in the mirror

turning it
into a hall
of mirrors

with strangers
projecting
fantasies,
good and evil

right there
on the same
face that
never posed,

or bothered
with fashion
in high school

the famous
face is shielded
now by Ray Bans

is pampered
at day spas
after hours

of rehearsal,
maneuvering,
campaigning,
cocaining~

the famous
body is starved,
squeezed into
tiny clothes
and watched
like a hawk

it is blatantly
on display,
or hidden
for lack of
perfection

every artificial
substance
that can mimic
good health is in
abundant supply

in the
compound
above the
city lights

the famous
one surrounded
now by handlers,
gigolos and users

engineering
the image,
the shoots,

the newsworthy
half-truths

twisting
vulnerable
youth about
what matters,
what is possible

the inner
circle which
on sober nights
one wonders
about~

may be
traitors
beneath
the loyalty

and the
paparazzi,
the public

who spy
and judge
and want
and envy
and copy
and worship
and scream
and mock
and expect
and dig for
dirt and
root for a
comeback
and relish
a scandal

and the secret
partners who
would not be in
this without the
glory, the
leap-frog
agenda

the
thing is~
fame itself
is a fickle
lover

and in the
end, you
may no
longer
know
yourself
when
loverless..

end game

laid out
on the grass
of a grand Esplanade

gutted
and sprawled out
on display
like a trophy

The Man has a
wide grin~
the conspiracy
is complete

no longer will he
be bothered
with excess
population

there's always
enough cheap
help to protect
that precious
bottom line

and it's all
good in the end
even to the last
forest, the
last winter,
the last shorebird

the last grandmother
the last baby shower
the last 50th

the helpless make
better workers
and they do not
question

they stay out of
his gated home,

and they know
their place

they know how to
stretch a dollar,
how to share,
how to sing in misery

they can string up
tarps in a flood
and live there
for months

they can do without
and when they can't,
they can grieve
their beloved dead
and keep moving

the Captain has
now gained the
rank of deity~
holding all the
secrets; predicting
the future

not bothered now
by newspaper critics~
blessed with
cozy government
agreements

he thinks, lives,
loves, breathes
on his island~
takes refuge
in his bunker

he has gained the
world and somehow
sees a soul
as a hindrance

the degraded,
abandoned world
is in his view
ready to be
traded in

he has his team of
scientists working
on that as we speak…

∽

strange game

what a strange card game
where belief is always
the trump suit

around the table
sit science,
history,
and statistics

they may be
boring, and
long-winded

they may be
poor listeners
and haughty

but the points
they make

are not disloyal
to the cause

the cause
being our
stewardship
of Mother Earth

and the
realism it will
take to scale
back

and learn to
thrive by
living in limits

learn to
cooperate with
diverse passengers
in the lifeboat

we believe
we can row
without them

living by
doctrine alone
and staying
apart

makes for
no real
conversation

only talk,
to rile us up
or pacify us

painting
pictures with
a broad brush

and teaching
fear, or worse,
of "the others"

leery of the
other players
at the table

because they
may not be
true believers

and having
the ultimate
back up plan

of promised
rewards upon
our death, or
the next election

we step back
from this table
and join our
friends

at their
table piled
high with
comfort food..

∞

assassins

the course of history
changed by
mad men

plotting to protect
their own access
to power

their own
wealth, their own
maniacal habits

like the Wall Street
swindler's
closet of shoes

there are
many ways to
assassinate

and one would
be to gain the
absolute faith

of those
whom you can
manipulate

and in the end
to treat it all
like a numbers game

denying the human
impact one
man's actions

can have on a
multitude of
lives, families

not to mention
the killing
aspect of

eroding the
fragile hold we
have on our
real assets..

those being
the things we
cannot see,
touch, or purchase..

∽

long walk with
a smoke

he walks
on the shoulder
of a busy road

plodding,
always looking
down

never seen
without his
cigarette

he is so
much like
our world

we want
it both
ways

we want
the
health

but we
want the
pleasure

we want
the
wealth

but we
don't want
sacrifice

we want
the
hope

but we
don't pay
attention

to what
we're
really
facing
up ahead

we seek
to
find

the
escape
hatch

we
don't
want to know

the
big
picture

we're not
told

about our
choices

and don't
want to
make them
anyway

we have
been
children

sitting
on
grandpa's
lap

waiting for
our story

and
grandpa
fell asleep

on his
generic
prescription...

still we wait,
not for tales of
truth, but for
that happy ending.

∽

the body politic

how cold
the shoulder
of exclusion

how evil
the eye
of revenge

how tin
the ear
of authority

how big
the mouth
of the gossip

how thumbed
the nose
of the snob

how curled
the pinkie
of the gentry

how jerked
the knees
of extremists

how sticky
the fingers
of lenders

how crossed
the palms
of officials

how blind
the eyes
of nonvoters

how vented
the spleens
of talking heads

how furrowed
the brows
of those
without work

how greased
the elbows
of workers

how burdened
the shoulders
of parents

how stiff
the upper lip
of those
growing old

how mealy
the mouths
of those
with excuses

how narrow
the view
of the
complacent

who will
step forward
to take hold
of our future?

and will we
be the
body politic,
one nation

tough enough
to proudly survive
a thousand cuts…

☙

for the reader

Thank you for reading this book. In a media-flooded world, it is a great honor to have you take the time to do this. I am interested in your response to my work, and welcome the opportunity to have a dialogue about these poems. For that purpose, I have set up a "like" page on Facebook, at Pamela Armstrong, PhD.

The web address featuring me as a poet/author is at www.drpamarmstrong.com I post on Twitter at Pamela Armstrong PhD. I am an active member at perfectnetworker.com, the dynamic social network where I first met Ken Rochon.

You may contact me directly at drpamarmstrong@gmail.com. I welcome your inquiries and ideas regarding future works.

More From Perfect Publishing

More From Perfect Publishing